stacey waite

the lake has no saint

TUPELO PRESS
NORTH ADAMS, MASSACHUSETTS

the lake has no saint
Copyright 2010 Stacey Waite. All rights reserved.
ISBN 978-1-932195-81-1

Cover and text designed by William Kuch, WK Graphic Design.
Cover art by gabrielle jesiolowski.
Printed in the United States.
First paperback edition: November 2010.

14 13 12   5 4

This book's epigraph quotes Ralph Angel's poem "Leaving One,"
from *Exceptions and Melancholies: Poems 1986–2006* (Sarabande Books, 2006).

No part of this book may be reproduced by any means without permission
of the publisher. Please address permissions requests to:

Tupelo Press
P.O. Box 1767, North Adams, Massachusetts 01247
Telephone: (413) 664-9611 / Fax: (413) 664-9711
editor@tupelopress.org / www.tupelopress.org

Tupelo Press is an award-winning independent literary press that publishes fine fiction, non-
fiction, and poetry in books that are a joy to hold as well as read. Tupelo Press is a registered
501(c)3 non-profit organization and relies on donations to carry out its mission of publishing
extraordinary work that may be outside the realm of large commercial publishers.

NATIONAL
ENDOWMENT
FOR THE ARTS

Supported in part by an award from
the National Endowment for the Arts

My staying here
would not protect you, these fingers
of yours, the soul in your shy eyes,
I'd simply go down trying.
We, right here, belong to us.
But I'm calling the shots now,
and now I'm leaving this hotel.
With all we've lost already
our pores are wide open.
And it's cold out there.
Come drive with me.

— from Ralph Angel's "Leaving One"

Contents

the lake

has no saint

when i do not want to say anything about the bridges

or about the land of sweet water where my mother
can not bear the shadows of light fixtures, she
can not bear the suburban quiet. her neighbor
sets raccoon traps beside the aspen tree,
which has been cut back away from windows.
there is little to say of the ocean which she can not
feel. i am not always sorry to return.
sometimes i imagine myself to the courtyard
of my high school. everyone is named "jodie"
or "rachel." the boys smoke around the flagpole
with their milk cartons and long hair. this is a
town with diners. no ravens, no steeples,
no hard rains. you wouldn't have liked it
though you wouldn't have known you didn't.
you can not put your feet in the ocean without
money. you can not learn or breathe without
money. you can not learn or breathe with
money—breathe without trains, without
becoming a mistress back in the horse trails
where the cut machines were sometimes kept.

when you are young there is no way of telling

yet your father suspects something about your walk, about the notes you write
to his secretary, lori. *i love you* you say *take me to the beach again* you say because
you are in fourth grade, because your father is in love with his nurse and not
your mother who can not bear to ease the dialysis needles in. she can not bear
anger or the color of dusk. *there is the waiting for someone else to die* your father says
the transplant wasn't much he says the first thing he does with his kidneys is *piss
on the operating table* he says laughing. and you are laughing too. you are thinking
about the tree fort your father had torn down. you do not think his piss is funny.
somewhere someone died you think *to save him.* when you imagine somewhere
someone died, he is always a good man, *someone who shouldn't have* you think,
though you would never say—just about your walk: you did not fall in love with
the secretary though once you took to smelling her hair and offering your breath
to the dry sand between her fingers.

when what is given breaks under

there is little of christmas i remember. one bicycle. my father's yellow whiskey. no snow, though i am sure there was. outside the long breath of my father's house, three distinct patches of lawn. on one, my brothers played "keep away" with the soccer ball. they would not let me touch it. on the two front lawns, we spent autumn stuffing black bags with the oak leaves. i was always the last one in. the last one dragged the bags to the street. it wasn't so much the being kept away or even the work of lifting the bags. mostly, it was the loneliness that got to me—the long dark lines of the back shed door.

when learning to be a boy

the neighbor boys look for frogs in the yard. i do not want them to find one. i want them to invent the game in which they are not looking for something to harm. i want them to invent the game in which they are not building villages they will bomb from their plastic planes. they make the bomb noises in unison. they fall down giggling in the grass until their mother names what has been cooking inside.

when you wish you had not said

still i can not forget the brown trim of the barn door and how still we were trapped in the thick fog of long island sky. my brother had been bitten in the face by a neighborhood dog who was, after all, put to sleep and i can't see as my brother would've gotten over such a thing—*that dog is dead now* my father says to my brother as if to make him feel better about the stitches. i do not remember my brother's face or the time it took to heal. it is possible i had not yet been born or been there or been born.

when saying *but i was not the kind of boy either*

who would tread the water of answering back, the boy who takes his young girlfriend to
the hayloft to kiss her among the smell of feed and shit; i would not take her there among
the feed and shit because i was not the kind of boy either who keeps for himself. this is the
woman who can not carry her body. she swallows the bindings of books, this bandaging.
she can not bear the stillness, can not keep the furniture, the bed how it is a city bed in
which lovers fail but i will not be the kind of boy who can not bear the memory of her body
aching as it will or won't once the burning once the ash carried out in the sheets which will
drift gray into the roads will not lead us away from the city nothing is taken in the hands.

when praying for gender

then there is my crying in dresses. "since i was born," my mother says. she walks the line of my crying. the church dress i will not. the pigtails i will not. the long nights praying: *please god, if you let me wake up and be a boy, i will never say another swear word again.*

when my grandfather dies in april

i dream he breathes out
candles in a dark hall
which feels like a tunnel
except for it's this house,
this hallway outside
the bedroom door.

i remember he says,
what small grace
and *there are places*
you can't bring this
kind of body. there's
a pitch black
to my following him,

always the hospital robe
always the last memory.

he wouldn't have known me
to make love to a woman
though, in the dream,
we seemed to recognize
each other with more precision,
with each lost flame.

there were times he'd lift me
up into trees. you can not
think of any specific kind
of tree but only it mustn't
be tied to the earth.

when feeling there is nowhere to turn

frostbitten. the boat in his hands is best and when she talks of tying up her hair. the poem i wrote in the attic will not on the surface seem best in this light the camera is of no use and the books we should not keep we should of course take them to someone who will read them, who will show up willing to pages. it always seems we are running. no one stops at anyone's door in this dream, the one with the taste of iron, where i can not even have breakfast in my own skin. the neighborhood does not rise to see like the lover who does not though she may rise—that is to fall.

when the chalk of androgyny

there was always something about the public bathroom doors, always the chalk of androgyny sticking in my throat as i'd walk towards the women's room with my mother. somehow i knew she wasn't bothered by the stick figure triangle skirt that indicated the path we were to take, the ways we were to interpret our bodies. but my mother and i do not have the same body. my mother does not read the doors at all; she is automatic in her automatic body. she tugs me in by my small arms and leads me to the stall. often, i have trouble urinating. i ask my mother to sing so no one will hear my body and she does. "i'm leavin' on a jetplane, don't know when i'll be back again . . . leavin' on a jetplane, don't know when i'll be back again."

when leaving the house as a man

i was sixteen the first time i saw a drag show. it was, as it turned out, my first time in a tie if we don't count the endless number of times i tried on my father's ties in the master bedroom, pulling each one close to my neck trying to learn how to loop the fabric, how to *become* a man. here, in this gay bar off the coast of suburban long island, drag queens called me "handsome," giggled when i pulled out their chairs and lit their cigarettes. and when i arrive home late, when i try to sneak in through the back sliding glass door, my mother sees me in the suit and tie. she, for a moment, covers her eyes as though i had been naked and not her child. "what are you doing?" she wants to know. "where could you have gone dressed like that?"

when loneliest in the mornings

last evening a wood crafter who makes chairs and beds from koa wood. fifteen monks have settled and worshipped in the temple since the year i was born. there are canyons. the ocean from their cavernous stomachs. hiking west and the last piece of sky folding over into dusk. i have always loved you this way despite our forgetting, despite some mornings how we leave one another quiet.

when an imposition of meaning

naming. kindergarten. i do not like salt water, the class gerbil or writing on the black board. i do not like the girls' line and the boys' line. i do not like swallowing my gum. i will not tell anyone my middle name. the teacher tells the whole class my middle name.

"it's ann," they scream, "we know it's ann."

don't count on it—was what my father used to say to mean no. the trees never mean it. they spit up fire. they sometimes think they can make stars. no one is there to deny them.

when someone asks if you believe what you just said

there are some stains only a dark rain can make. somewhere my father holds the door for two women carrying green vines he can not name out from the grocery. this is mostly what he has to offer. i can not build lives for myself in the city. the book shelves are weighing on me. the candlewax two months hardened. i can not answer telephones or letters or for others dreaming is a different kind of epistemology elbowing its way through the bar we used to sneak in through the back where the cocktail waitresses gathered to smoke and say *fuck you*. i can not make my lover happy. i can not sweep more floors in the wood house. i used to touch the neighbor boy in the hayloft though we didn't mean anything by it except the way one means to peel a lemon in summer when we need it most the rain won't seem to arrive when i want to go back to the house. it's still the same now to touch—save for the element of danger. but it's all the body's worry. the landscape has no say. he was a drummer that neighbor boy, became someone big i believe though my father never liked him. didn't trust him he said, the way he'd open the cabinets in a foreign home, the way he'd sometimes throw sand down my shirt, the way he'd put his hands around my neck and pretend to strangle me *for practice* he'd say, *if someone ever bothered you* he'd laugh. he'd say *and what if he has you like this?*

when you are thinking about the vineyard city as waiting

no moon january. my lover, after taking her hand from my body, gives the death toll in thailand. she is thinking again about the lost houses. her friend has given her beads for her wrist. it's true i am lonely mostly in the mornings. sometimes i am thinking of something else. for instance, in the afternoon, my mouth pressed into the pull of her body, i am thinking of the still river in ohio, among the fallen trees, how i was ecstatic to touch her breasts so close to the deer. some days we just have lunch. she buys me a sweater. cut hair. the diligent day errands. there's no way to tell really. what we will need. what body will come forward as if to say *hear me i am not asking for anything.*

when in a cabin in maine

no room where the fish
were sometimes cut
no claw foot tub
in which to wring
out the sorrow
from her body
we swim the length
of the lake apart
last night her hand
drafts my body
in halves
we do not keep
the records
of what has been lost
she says she would
again if not for
wanting to see underwater
and my body is underwater
the bed is underwater
her hand heavy
in the wet shell
of another summer
in maine no the fish
were not cut in this room
in this room the fish
were not cut or taken
from underwater
the room itself is

underwater
the bed is underwater
the body the cut trees
the wreckage of towns
all taken under
the lake
has no saint
after which
to take its name

when in spring the self-pity

you would not like the way i have taken to living though i've much to say about the tree branches how i would collect them as a child to burn in what was called the "fire pit" though i had always wished it called something else. father, in the split house i will learn to boil okra pods until they are tender until they have bled themselves into a thick stew because i try to be good the way it is good to prepare to cut the yard vines back from the windows to keep from breaking the glass will break the latches the split slates of roof. i have not been paying close attention and soon the house will be lost.

when after you have exhausted the possibilities

blank the sun does not matter the jeweled edges of your body do not matter not in the
spring which arrives late in the evening i will not paint the new house blue i will not paint
the new house blue somewhere she is walking in fields and when i do not paint the new
house blue she will not weep for her mother for what she has lost and calls to report lost
the news of dying you do not understand but will not paint the new house blue no wall no
roof no blue in the ceilings or gutters blue is not the color you will paint the new house
though your body blue though your hands blue as what comes before a bruise she says what
wood will not lie beneath the haunted bed.

when in winter you bring home white lilies

some time later
she washes the blood
from the white sheets

we cook the rice softer this time
we eat less of it
we lean out the window
into the city rivers
how they wrap us
in their water arms

when bearing the burden of this sound

of a chainsaw out in the distant trees

      a man cuts what is left twisted from wind. he holds out the blade to deep fog and watches shreds of root pull back to his reddening face and here in the wood house my mouth pressed to the warm calm inside you. we know we can not breathe out what others can hear.

we keep quiet in the small room
your body leaning into my jawbone

when you can not remember the last time

which may or may not have been rough or good or flushing through the vines of this house or when she pulled them in from outside. it is true that she pulled the vines into the house through the upstairs window the neighbors have heard us moving into one another's bodies though we could not hear them watching. the books from their cases are drowning in what they might have said if not for the vines. what brings us there safe wanting and again to the solid earth which is not true though she'd like to believe in the failure of the city to hold up its bridges she says it is not enough for the body to give.

when during the hail storm, no light

i can not find the bread. i can not find the floorboards or their brown handles. sometimes the lake is more sound than voices or more sound than a paddle entering the water. i have a dream she says, *i should have loved you,* and she pulls green stems from the ground and she leans back into the earth and she asks me to pull down the ladder, to walk up into the light.

when it is becoming more difficult to yield and respond

this isn't the first time you've slept through my crying, though i am comforted by the thought of a vine that could fill the lake, *turn it into a swamp* she says in the cabin in july how the residents fear its spreading from the bottom of the boats that mostly have motors, and blue stripes, and flags. it is becoming more difficult to see, to move in the widening heat. we will not mail this letter to your mother. i lose you out in the lake though no vines to mention, no wind or sky.

when first to say i am sorry i am not at this point able to build what architects

there are moments, though, we forget our identity. we are laughing over gin and the story of your volkswagen floor. we put potato peels in the compost because you are the kind of woman who will not abandon is how it feels to hear you from the hospital in johnstown or from the house and its long vines. then you say to me *it is not your fault that your mother is lonely.* it is moving into winter. long highway, your daughter asleep in the backseat. you are driving towards what's left of ohio's fields.

when after she guides my fingers

out from the red memory of her body,
she turns away toward the window
screen holding up the shadows
of vines. it's even possible she's
conjuring up an old ship harbor
on the coast of maine or whispering
to herself of the stone steps down
to the cellar. we've ended up here before,
no curtains to soften the quickness
of morning sun, no frame for the bed.
if we need it badly enough, i suppose.
if we need. if we pull up
the nails from the attic floor.

when my body shaven clean in the white room

i imagine tying your wrists to the oak bed
i imagine your body in summer
how it leans into the earth
how it pulls back from the canvas
to breathe: it's not easy to know
when you've forgotten me
or when the trees come up
from their roots. i've put out
a birdfeeder, i've hung prayer flags
from the roof of the house.
i've turned over the soil
in the flowerbeds. please.
there isn't any more
i could ask of you.

Acknowledgments

Black Warrior Review — "when after you have exhausted the possibilities"

Cream City Review — "when in spring the self-pity"

Encyclopedia Destructica — "when after she guides my fingers"

Gulf Stream — "when someone asks if you believe what you just said"

Interim — "when you can not remember the last time"

Knockout — The following poems appeared as part of a longer poem called "Trans": "when learning to be a boy," "when leaving the house as a man," "when praying for gender," "when the chalk of androgyny"

Other books from Tupelo Press

This Lamentable City, Polina Barskova,
      edited and introduced by Ilya Kaminsky
This Nest, Swift Passerine, Dan Beachy-Quick
Cloisters, Kristin Bock
Stone Lyre: Poems of René Char,
      translated by Nancy Naomi Carlson
Poor-Mouth Jubilee, Michael Chitwood
staring at the animal, John Cross
Psalm, Carol Ann Davis
The Flight Cage, Rebecca Dunham
Then, Something, Patricia Fargnoli
Calendars, Annie Finch
Other Fugitives & Other Strangers, Rigoberto González
The Us, Joan Houlihan
Dancing in Odessa, Ilya Kaminsky
Ardor, Karen An-hwei Lee
Biogeography, Sandra Meek
Flinch of Song, Jennifer Militello
At the Drive-In Volcano, Aimee Nezhukumatathil
The Beginning of the Fields, Angela Shaw
The Forest of Sure Things, Megan Snyder-Camp
Human Nature, Gary Soto
Archicembalo, G.C. Waldrep
Dogged Hearts, Ellen Doré Watson
The Book of Whispering in the Projection Booth,
      Joshua Marie Wilkinson
Narcissus, Cecilia Woloch
Monkey Lightning, Martha Zweig

See our complete backlist at www.tupelopress.org